Three For The Third Day

Three Easter Sunrise Services

Mary Lu Warstler

CSS Publishing Company, Inc.
Lima, Ohio

THREE FOR THE THIRD DAY

Copyright © 1995 by
CSS Publishing Company, Inc.
Lima, Ohio

All rights reserved. If you are the original purchaser you may copy the bulletin material which appears on pages 11, 22-23, and 36-37. No other part of this publication may be reproduced, stored in a retrieval system, or transmitted in any form or by any means, electronic, mechanical, photocopying, recording, or otherwise, without the prior permission of the publisher. Inquiries should be addressed to: CSS Publishing Company, Inc., 517 South Main Street, P.O. Box 4503, Lima, Ohio 45802-4503.

Scripture quotations are from the *New Revised Standard Version of the Bible,* copyright 1989, by the Division of Christian Education of the National Council of the Churches of Christ in the USA. Used by permission.

ISBN 0-7880-0331-3   PRINTED IN U.S.A.

*In appreciation of the Seekers Class:
Wilda, Cora, Ruth, Joanne,
Anne, Sandy,
and John.*

Table Of Contents

Preface   7

Part 1   We Were There!   9
   Bulletin   11
   Instructions   12
   We Were There!   13

Part 2   A Night Of Memories   21
   Bulletin   22
   Instructions   24
   A Night Of Memories   27

Part 3   The Dream   35
   Bulletin   36
   Instructions   38
   The Dream   41

Preface

It seems that a lot of plays and pageants are written around the Christmas story. It is so easy to capture the mood of birth and life. But Easter plays or sunrise services are harder to find for some reason.

I think that is partly because we find it difficult to speak of death — even when we know the end of the story! I think, too, that it is easier to involve children in the Christmas story. Everyone loves the "little angels" of Christmas. Death and rising again is more adult oriented in our thinking.

And I suppose there is that element of triumph and spectacular joy with the Easter Service which we are often reluctant to have overshadowed or "upstaged" by telling the story at the sunrise service.

But I think that the story needs to be told over and over and over again in order for it to become a part of who we are.

These three short plays and music programs are attempts to give some variety to the Easter sunrise — or simply early service of Easter since most of us do not really have a "sunrise" service.

Part 1

We Were There

(For Printed Bulletin)

Easter Sunrise Service
We Were There!
by
Mary Lu Warstler

Prelude

Scripture Matthew 27:62-66

Prayer

Hymn "What Wondrous Love"

Scene 1
The Women's Report

Hymn "Were You There?"

Scene 2
Mary Magdalene Returns

Hymn "Christ The Lord Is Risen Today"

Benediction

Postlude

Instructions

Introduction

This sunrise service is based on the story of Mary Magdalene's visit to the bomb. As several women sit together wondering about the events that have occurred, three women who have been to the tomb come and tell them that the Lord is risen. Then they hear Mary Magdalene's story of how her life had been changed by meeting Jesus.

Playing time — approximately 30 minutes

Costumes

Traditional biblical dress or simply shawls or sheets held like shawls.

Scenery

The three (or more) women are seated informally in a room with a small table, a chair and small stools. This arrangement is used for both scenes.

Characters

Martha
Mary Magdalene
Salome
Mary 1 (Jesus' mother)
Mary 2 (Martha's sister)
Mary 3 (James' mother)
(More can be added without speaking parts.)

All characters can be played by adults, teens or older elementary children.

We Were There!

Prelude

Scripture Matthew 27:62-66

Prayer

Hymn "What Wondrous Love"

Scene 1
The Women's Report

Mary 1: Look! There are some women running this way. It looks like Mary Magdalene and Salome and someone else — I can't quite make out who. Quickly, open the door. Something has happened. Let them in.

Martha: Yes, it is Mary Magdalene and Salome and Mary, Little James' mother.

(Three women enter from center aisle.)

Mary 2: What is it? What has happened?

Mary M: Let us catch our breath, first.

(The three women sit down. Everyone speaks at once asking questions.)

Mary 1: Give them time. Let them begin to tell their story when they are ready.

Mary M: He is not there. He is risen as he said he would.

Martha: What do you mean, "He is not there"? Who is not where? Where have you been so early in the morning?

(All begin again asking questions at once.)

Mary M: Wait, I can't hear when you all talk at once.

Mary 1: She is right, of course. Let her begin at the beginning.

Mary M: Mary and Salome and I went to the tomb while it was still dark. We were afraid of being caught, but we thought if we were there at daybreak, we could have our prayers of sorrow and maybe anoint our Lord since we could not do it earlier.

Martha: What about the stone? How did you think you would be able to move it? And even if you did, wouldn't there be an odor?

Mary 1: Yes, what about the stone?

Mary 3: We thought about that. We were afraid that we would not be able to roll the stone away.

Salome: Even if we were not caught, it would do us no good to be there if the stone were in the way.

Mary 3: We almost decided not to go. But then we thought that if we could not roll the stone away we could still go. We would leave our spices and ointments outside beside the stone. We would pray and then go back to our homes.

Mary M: But when we got there the stone was gone! How foolish we had been to worry so needlessly! The guards were nowhere to be seen.

Salome: We were really frightened then. But we refused to turn back until we had found out what was going on.

Mary 2: Did you go inside the tomb?

Mary 3: Yes, we went inside thinking we may as well do what we came to do. We saw a young man sitting there dressed in a white robe.

Martha: An angel? You saw an angel?

Salome: Yes, I suppose that is who he was. I didn't think we could be more frightened than we were on our way to the tomb, but at that minute I knew what it meant to be paralyzed with fear.

Mary 3: That's right. We thought maybe we were in the wrong place.

Mary M: But, I was so sure it was the right place. I thought the man in white was one of the guards — although it was strange dress for a guard. We thought maybe they had moved Jesus. I was beginning to tremble. I think Mary and Salome were too.

Salome: Yes, I just knew we would all be arrested.

Mary M: We saw the empty bed of stone and the man in the white robe sitting there. As we glanced at each other, we did not have to say a word. We each knew what the other was thinking. Slowly we started backing away from the tomb, hoping to run before he caught us. The man spoke and the sound of his voice was so different — I can't really describe it.

Mary 3: Like golden bells.

Salome: Or like the ripple of a rushing brook.

Mary M: The thought passed through my mind that he might be an angel, but I thought that was impossible.
    He spoke to us. He asked why we were there and who we were looking for. He said, "Surely you are not looking

for Jesus of Nazareth who was crucified. Why would you look for the living among the dead? He is not here. He has risen!"

Then he told us not to stand there with our mouths open but to go and tell Peter and the rest what we saw. Well, we didn't need to be told a second time. We turned and ran as fast as we could. We came here to tell you what we had heard and seen.

Mary 3: He did say he would be raised from the dead in three days. But we don't know where he is.

Mary 1: Did you tell Peter and John?

Mary M: No, we came here first.

Mary 1: Then let us go tell them now.

(All exit.)

Hymn "Were You There?"

Scene 2
Mary Magdalene Returns

(The women, except Mary Magdalene, are all gathered in the same place. They are talking among themselves — wondering where Mary Magdalene is.)

Salome: Where is Mary Magdalene?

Mary 3: She was here a little while ago.

Martha: You don't suppose she went back there, do you?

Salome: I don't know. She was pretty upset. She just might want to see it again.

Mary 1: Maybe we should go look for her.

Mary 2: I don't know. Maybe we ought to get Peter and John. Let them go search for her.

Martha: Oh, look. Here she comes now.

(Mary Magdalene enters from the center aisle.)

Salome: There you are. Where have you been? We were beginning to worry about you. We were getting ready to search for you.

Mary M: I'm sorry. I didn't mean to alarm anyone. I just needed to go back. It is all so hard to believe. I had to reassure myself that it was all true — that the tomb is empty.

I slipped out while you were talking and went back to the tomb. I wasn't afraid anymore — not of the guards or the angel. At least I tried to tell myself that I wasn't afraid. I just wanted to see the empty tomb again. I could not believe what was happening.

When I returned to the place of the tomb, it was still true. No one was there — not even the angel! I just stood for a while, thinking and trying to understand.

(Mary pauses then continues.)

I could not stop the tears. They just kept spilling over my eyes and down my face. I probably look pretty awful. The memories kept coming in torrents just like the tears — memories that I thought I had forgotten.

Mary 1: Do you want to share it with us?

Mary M: *(She pauses then continues.)* Yes, somehow I feel it is important to share my story with you. As I stood there looking at that empty tomb, I remembered how I had been possessed. Seven demons had possessed my mind and body. Not knowing where my life was headed, I just tried to live from day to day. With every rising sun I hoped my mind and body would cooperate and let me live a normal life. Many days I really did not care if I lived or died. More often than not I preferred to die, but I lacked the courage to do anything about it.

When I first saw Jesus, I wondered what kind of man he was. A carpenter from Nazareth, the people had said. How could he do all the things they said he had done and was doing? He did not look very strong and powerful from a distance. But then he came closer. I felt my body begin to convulse and I just knew that I would do something dumb or strange or embarrassing. I wanted to hide, but his eyes met mine and I could not move. He stopped in front of me and held out his hand. I placed my hand in his and the tears began to flow. I knew the strangeness was gone forever. The demons left me. They no longer controlled my body and mind.

I loved Jesus from the bottom of my heart with a love that only could be from God. I would have gone to the ends of the earth for him, as I know all of you would. And yet there I was at the tomb and I couldn't even find his body to weep over and properly mourn. As I stood there remembering the past, the reality of the present became more fearful. I wanted to go back inside but found that I could not move. Clinging to the side of the tomb, grief consumed me and I wept. When I thought I could look again, I stooped to go in. This time I saw two angels who asked why I was crying.

(Mary pauses.)

Salome: Go on, we want to hear everything.

Mary M: I heard a sound behind me. Turning, I saw a man. Through the blur of tears in my eyes, I thought he was the gardener. "Why are you crying?" he asked. "Who are you looking for?"

The voice was so familiar, but I would not let my mind hear what my heart was saying. Somehow I managed to control the sound of my voice. I said, "I am looking for the body of Jesus who was laid in this tomb. He is not here and I don't know where they have taken him. I wanted to anoint the body. Sir, do you know where they have taken him? Do you know where the body is now?"

I thought maybe this gardener had put him some place else. And then he smiled at me. And then ... then he spoke my name. For a split second I think my heart stopped beating. I thought I must be dreaming. Maybe the demons were back — playing tricks with my mind. I said, "Teacher? Master?" Our eyes met and I knew. I fell at his feet, but he would not let me touch him.

"Do not cling to me," he said. "I have not yet ascended to my Father and your Father, to my God and your God."

I was so overjoyed and yet so pained. I wanted so much to touch him, to know that he was real — not just my imagination. I wanted to believe everything would be the same as before. But I knew that would never be.

Mary 1: He is really alive? You have really seen him?

Mary M: Yes, Mary, he is really alive! I have seen him. I have talked to him. I thought I was full of joy when he cleansed me and made me whole. I thought I could never love him more than I did then, but when I saw him in the garden, I knew my life was changing again.

Isn't it strange — in a wonderful sort of way — that every time we meet Jesus something happens and our lives become different? He is indeed alive. And because he lives, we too shall live — truly live.

I wanted to stay there in that garden with him. I wanted to hear his plans and his goals for my life. I just wanted to sit at his feet and hear about all the stories he had to tell. Especially, I wanted to hear about those three days in the grave. But he said he must go. I had to be content that he had been there and that I would see him again.

I came back to tell you that I had seen our Lord. We will have to leave this place and the comfort of our fellowship together. We will come together for strength and courage and worship — but the real work is out there for each one of us. Christ our Lord has risen this day! We, too, must rise up and follow him.

Christ the Lord is risen today! Come let us sing his praise!

(All exit.)

Hymn "Christ The Lord Is Risen Today"

Benediction

Postlude

This play is based on a story in Chapter 10 from *Before The Dawn: A Night Of Memories* by Mary Lu Warstler copyright 1993. Scripture references from the New Revised Standard Version of the Holy Bible, the Gospel of John.

Part 2

A Night Of Memories

(For Printed Bulletin)

A Night Of Memories
by
Mary Lu Warstler

Prelude

Opening Prayer

Welcome and Announcements

Offering

Doxology

Hymn "Were You There?"

A Night Of Memories
Jesus has been crucified and laid in a tomb. The time of Passover and Unleavened Bread is over. Mary, the mother of Jesus, is waiting for the sun to rise so that she can go with the other women to take spices to the tomb and say their final farewell. As she sits in her chair by the window, scenes from the past begin to enter her memory.

Scene 1
The Angel's Visit

Hymn "In The Garden" (Verse 1)

Scene 2
Sharing The News

Hymn "There's A Song In The Air" (Verse 1)

Scene 3
A Child Is Born

Hymn "Silent Night" (verse 1)

Scene 4
In The Temple

Hymn "This Is My Father's World" (Verse 1)

Hymn "Ah, Holy Jesus" (Verse 1)

Scene 5
Hosanna! Hosanna!

Hymn "Hosanna"

Scene 6
It Is Finished

Hymn " 'Tis Finished! The Messiah Dies"

Scene 7
A New Day Dawns

Hymn "Christ The Lord Is Risen Today"

Benediction

Postlude

Instructions

Introduction

This sunrise service is a reminder of the life of Christ as seen from the perspective of his mother, Mary.

It involves as many persons as are wanted or as few as two, depending on the size of the congregation. The congregation is involved in singing the hymns. Usually only the first verse of each hymn will be sufficient, but all can be used if you want.

The main character is Mary, the mother of Jesus, who is sitting alone on the night before the Third Day, just remembering and pondering all that has taken place since the first angel's visit in Bethlehem.

Playing time — approximately 30 minutes

Costumes

Mary is dressed as a biblical woman would have been dressed. An easy way would be to use a sheet (pale blue) folded and draped over the head held with a band and the rest held like a shawl around her.

The others are dressed in traditional biblical costumes.

Scenery

Mary is seated throughout the play. She is in a comfortable chair close to a "window" or pretend window. There can be a table with a candle on it and maybe a ceramic cup and pitcher.

The scenes within the scene can be done either with live action and characters speaking their parts, or with characters only acting out the part and a narrator reading their parts, or with shadow-type tableaus. These scenes should be portrayed off to one side of Mary (whatever way she is facing) and, if possible, more toward the congregation.

Characters

Mary (remains seated until the end of the last scene)
Angel
Younger Mary
Elizabeth
Joseph
Boy Jesus
Children with palm branches (can use many or only one as a symbol of many)
Two Women (who have been to the tomb)
Narrator (only if you do not use the other characters)

Mary should be played by an older teen or an adult. The "scenes within the scene" or "tableaus" can be played by older elementary children. If a narrator is used instead of children speaking parts, that person should be an adult or older teen.

A Night Of Memories

Prelude

Opening Prayer

Welcome and Announcements

Offering

Doxology

Hymn "Were You There?"

A Night Of Memories
Jesus has been crucified and laid in the tomb. The time of Passover and Unleavened Bread is over. Mary, the mother of Jesus, is waiting for the sun to rise so that she can go with the other women to take spices to the tomb and say their final farewell. As she sits in her chair by the window, scenes from the past begin to enter her memory.

Scene 1
The Angel's Visit

(Mary is seated in a chair either by a pretend window or a prop made to look like a window.)

Mary: *(Looking around the room as she talks.)* The Sabbath is almost over. It has been a long day. John has been so kind, but I am glad to be alone for a while. So much has happened. So many things to think about and to ponder. I need to just think. *(Leans her head back and just sits for a few seconds. Then she wipes tears from her eyes.)* I know I must face the awful truth. I know that once the day breaks, I must go with the others to the tomb to make the arrangements for a proper burial, but for now I must just sit here and think. I must let the tears flow if they will. Yes, I will just sit here and remember. Remembrance! Oh, how sweet and yet so bitter. Has it been so long? Or was it just yesterday? Time has lost all meaning for me *(Pause.)* Was there really an angel or did I just imagine it? No, I am sure it was true. I was so frightened. It was true all right. I can still see that angel as if it were just yesterday. He was so tall and so ... so sparkling white. *(Closes her eyes and leans back in the chair.)*

Congregation "In The Garden" (Verse 1)

(Scene of Mary in the Garden.)

Angel: Don't be afraid, Mary. You have found favor with God. You will conceive and bear a son, and you will call him Jesus. He will be great! He will be called the Son of the Most High.[1]

Mary: How can this be? I am not yet married.

Angel: The Holy Spirit will come upon you and the power of the Most High will overshadow you. Therefore, the child to be born will be called holy, the Son of God.[2]

Mary: Behold, I am the handmaid of the Lord; let it be to me according to your word.[3]

Scene 2
Sharing The News

(Scene again returns to Mary alone in her chair.)

Mary: No! It was not a dream. *(Smiles as she remembers.)* I remember thinking and wondering how I could ever face dear, sweet Joseph and my friends. But how gentle and loving he was. He understood. He loved me even when people misunderstood. Yes, it was all true. That same angel told me about Elizabeth — that she was pregnant, too. I could hardly believe it. Elizabeth! Why she had to have been as old as Sarah. I could hardly wait until I could go to her and see for myself. The Lord filled me with a song that I just had to sing. Oh, I wish I could sing it now. *(Bows her head in her hands as Mary and Elizabeth meet in the tableau scene.)*

Music Chorus of "His Eye Is On The Sparrow"

Mary: Elizabeth! An angel has just told me the news. I am so happy for you. After all these years of waiting, God has blessed you with a child.

Elizabeth: Blessed are you among women. And blessed is the child which you bear. But why has it been granted to me to see the mother of our Lord?[4]

Mary: My soul magnifies the Lord, and my spirit rejoices in God my Savior for he has regarded the lowly estate of his handmaiden.[5]

Congregation "There's A Song In The Air" (Verse 1)

Scene III
A Child Is Born

(Scene returns to Mary in her chair. She lifts her arms to God as in prayer.)

Mary: I don't understand what has happened. You said he was your Son and that he would be the Messiah, the Savior of our people. Have I misunderstood? Did I fail to do the will of Yahweh? Are you punishing me for some wrong that I did without knowing? Wasn't this to be the Messiah, the Redeemer? *(Voice* *trails off on the end of the word.)* Will my life ever be the same? Will it ever be normal again? Oh, Lord my God, I know I will go on. I know that you are God. But for now, what can I do? He was my son. He was a good baby. Even in that cold, drafty old stable.

(Mary, Joseph, manger, shepherds, wise men, angels, or as many or as few beyond Mary and Joseph and the manger as you want to use. Remain silently in place while congregation sings.)

Congregation "Silent Night" (Verse 1)

Scene 4
In The Temple

(Return to Mary in her chair.)

Mary: *(Smiles as she remembers.)* Yes, those were hard days, but oh, the joy of holding that precious infant in my arms! *(Folds arms as if holding a baby.)* The shepherds who came were so rugged and smelled of sheep. And kings, too. I had never seen such royalty — and to think they came to see MY baby! *(Pause)* If only they could be here now! What would they think?

(Pauses, then continues smiling to herself.) I remember the little rascal when he was a toddler, hanging onto my skirt tail, following me around the house, dragging out my cooking pans. Oh, the noise he could make with them! And, oh, the trees that boy used to climb. He roamed the mountains so often that I was sure he would get lost, until I realized that God was taking care of him. But still, I couldn't quite grasp what he was saying that time in the temple.

Congregation "This Is My Father's World" (Verse 1)

(The boy Jesus is at the center of the chancel. Mary and Joseph come down the center aisle.)

Mary: Hurry, Joseph. We must hurry! Oh, my poor baby. Where can he be? We have looked everywhere.

Joseph: Now, Mary. Try to stay calm. You know how curious he is. I'm sure he will be all right. We must trust Yahweh to guide us to him.

Mary: I know, I know. But I can't help worrying. I just ... *(Sees Jesus in the temple.)* There he is! There he is! *(Runs to him and puts arms around him.)* There you are! Are you all right? Oh, you naughty boy! Didn't you know we would be worried about you? Don't you know we have looked three days for you? We were scared to death!

Jesus: *(Sounding surprised)* Why, Mother! Didn't you know I must be about my Father's business?[6]

(Mary and Joseph pause and look at their son. Then take his hand.)

Mary: Come, Jesus. Let us go home for now.

(Leave down center aisle — or the way they came in.)

Congregation "Ah, Holy Jesus" (Verse 1)

Scene 5
Hosanna! Hosanna!

(Return to Mary in her chair.)

Mary: Is this what he meant? *(Raising her eyes toward heaven.)* Is this the business he had to be about? Did it have to end this way? *(Pauses briefly.)* He really did love life. He had so much fun. The wedding feast in Cana — oh, that was such a beautiful time ... and the wine he made from water. I still don't understand how or why he did it. And all those people he healed. Where are they now? Just last week — was it really only a week? — he rode into Jerusalem on the back of a little donkey. How proud I was! That was MY son they were honoring. All those people who lined the streets and shouted "Hosanna! Hosanna!" I thought that he was really the Messiah and had come to save our people. We all thought he would make everything right again.

(Children with palm branches enter as congregation sings.)

Congregation "Hosanna"

Scene 6
It Is Finished

(Return to Mary in her chair.)

Mary: How quickly they changed their tune! They called *him* a common criminal! How could they have crucified him? How could *(Voice gets softer.)* he have been so quiet, so forgiving? "Father, forgive them. They don't know what they are doing," he said.[7]

(Sounding puzzled.) I wonder what he meant when he told the one thief that he would see him in paradise. Was he, too, not guilty of any wrong? And dear John. He loved Jesus so much. And now John will have to be my arm to lean on.

I wish I could understand. He said he was the Messiah. He said he would be raised in three days. But, I just don't understand. Why did he have to die in the first place? He should not have died.

(A wooden cross is carried down the center aisle.)

Congregation " 'Tis Finished! The Messiah Dies"

Scene 7
A New Day Dawns!

(Return to Mary in her chair.)

Mary: What is that? The sun rising already? Soon the others will be here. I must go and say goodbye for the last time. Can it really be the last time? Somehow I feel that something has changed. He did say he would come back. Isn't that what he said? He never lied to me before. He will keep his word! I don't know how, but I know that he will return.

(She begins to show more excitement as the truth begins to dawn upon her.) The sun is getting higher. It is so bright! So bright it reminds me of that night so long ago when a star . . . *(Awareness of truth shows as she smiles.)* It is true. It is true! God has provided the way as he said he would. It is over. It is truly over. Death is no more. He has overcome it! I know that somehow he has overcome it.

(Pianist/organist begins playing softly "Christ The Lord Is Risen Today" as two women begin moving excitedly down the center aisle. They are speaking to each other with excitement as they hurry along. They reach Mary and begin explaining to her.)

First: He is not there! We went to the tomb early. He is not there!

Second: An angel was there. He said he has risen.

Mary: *(Standing)* Yes, I know. I know! He has risen! He said he would! Remember? The grave could not hold him. Death has lost its grip. Oh, my soul does truly magnify the Lord, and my spirit rejoices in God, my savior . . . He has helped his servant Israel . . . He has risen! He has risen! He has risen!

Congregation "Christ The Lord Is Risen Today"

Benediction

Postlude

Parts of Mary's monologue are taken from Chapter 9 of *Before The Dawn: A Night Of Memories* by Mary Lu Warstler, copyright 1993.

Scripture quotes are from the New Revised Standard Version of the Holy Bible.

---

1. Luke 1:30-32a

2. Luke 1:35

3. Luke 1:38

4. Luke 1:42b-43

5. Luke 1:47-48

6. Luke 2:49

7. Luke 23:34

Part 3

The Dream

(For Printed Bulletin)

The Dream
by
Mary Lu Warstler

Prelude

Call To Worship

Invocation

Hymn "What Wondrous Love Is This?"

The Dream

Scene 1

Hymn "At The Cross"

Scene 2

Hymn "Surely He Bore Our Grief"
or "Alas! And Did My Savior Bleed"

Scene 3

Hymn " 'Tis Midnight And On Olive's Brow"

Scene 4

Hymn "The Strife Is O'er, The Battle Done"

Scene 5

Hymn "In The Garden"

Scene 6

Hymn "Christ The Lord Is Risen Today!"
or "Low In The Grave He Lay"

Benediction

Postlude

Instructions

Introduction

This drama is about two contemporary friends who have been friends for a long time. They have shared a lot of discussions. Joe is a Christian, but his friend Sam is not. Sam doesn't even want to discuss religion — and especially not Christianity. But Joe never gives up.

The story is woven in and around many of the Lenten and Easter hymns. In the drama I have indicated that they be sung by a choir. However, they may be sung by the congregation or various combinations — solos, duets, choir, and congregation.

The scenery is simple, as are the costumes. On Easter Sunday morning no one wants to spend a lot of time getting in and out of costumes. If you prefer, this drama can be used on a Sunday evening during Lent.

Hymns Used

"At The Cross"
"Surely He Bore Our Grief"
   or "Alas! And Did My Savior Bleed"
" 'Tis Midnight And On Olive's Brow"
"The Strife Is O'er, The Battle Done"
"In The Garden"
"Christ The Lord Is Risen Today"
   or "Low In The Grave He Lay"

Scenery

There is only one setting — Sam's living room. In this room you will need one or two comfortable chairs, a small table with a phone on it. You may add any other items that you wish, but I suggest you keep it simple and let the congregation use its imagination. Other props you will need: box of crackers, glass of milk, ball and bat, and catcher's mitt.

Costumes

Sam and Joe are in their regular modern clothes — jacket and baseball-type hat — In the first half of the first scene. The rest of the play, Joe is in a white robe with wings. Isaiah wears a rough-looking robe. Mary Magdalene can wear a choir robe or a pastel-colored sheet folded and draped over her head and shoulders like a shawl. The choir may be robed or simply wear church clothes.

Characters

Joe (young adult or teen)
Sam (young adult or teen)
Isaiah (Prophet from the Old Testament)
Mary Magdalene (from the New Testament)
Choir and/or Congregation

All characters can be played by adults, teens or older elementary children.

The Dream

Prelude

Call To Worship

Hymn "What Wondrous Love"

Scene 1

(Sam and Joe enter from one side of the stage. Joe is carrying his catcher's mitt. Sam is carrying a ball and bat. He sets the ball and bat down and removes his jacket, throwing it across one of the chairs.)

Sam: Take off your coat and stay a while.

Joe: No, I have to get home. When are your parents getting home?

Sam: Sometime tomorrow if Gramps is feeling better. Say, that was a good game today, wasn't it? The weather was perfect. No rain for a change.

Joe: Yes, wasn't it a glorious day? Didn't God give us such beauty today?

Sam: *(Frowning)* Look, Joe, we've been friends a long time and you know how I feel about that religious stuff. So knock it off. Sure, it's a beautiful day, but not because God made it.

Joe: Then who did?

Sam: No one. It just is what it is. That's all. I suppose your God made the thunderstorm we had last week, too!

(Sam pushes his hands deep into his pockets and turns away before his friend can answer him.)

Joe: Well, I gotta go. See you soon, and may God grant you rest. *(Leaves same way they entered.)*

Sam: *(To himself)* Phooey, I'm too tired to listen to his nonsense.

(Goes off stage and returns carrying box of crackers and glass of milk.)

Sam: I wish Mom and Dad were here. I'm too tired to even think of fixing a meal.

(Sits in chair, leans back and relaxes.)

I think I'll just sit here for a while and eat these crackers and milk.

(Sits in chair, eats crackers, drinks milk for a while. Then begins to nod off.)

(Joe enters dressed in white robe and wings.)

Joe: Come here. Look. *(Points out window.)* See that little white church. Listen to the choir sing.

(Sam gets up and looks in the direction Joe is pointing.)

(Music begins softly playing "At The Cross" gradually getting louder as curtain falls — or Joe and Sam leave the stage.)

Choir "At The Cross"

Scene 2

(Music fades away as curtain rises. Joe and Sam are back in the living room.)

Joe: Wasn't that beautiful? Did you ever hear anything so nice?

Sam: *(Sarcastically)* Yeah. Very nice. *(Turns to go back to his chair but can only move in slow motion.)*

(Isaiah enters and stands quietly to one side behind the boys.)

Joe: Wait, come with me and meet some folks.

Sam: Do I have a choice?

Joe: It's your dream, pal. You can wake up whenever you want.

Sam: Oh, all right, let's go. But I warn you. If you start too much of that religious stuff, I'll open my eyes and you'll be gone.

Joe: Fine. Come on over here. I want you to meet my friend, Isaiah.

Sam: You mean that scruffy looking guy over there? *(Points to where Isaiah is standing.)*

Joe: Yeah. You remember I told you about how he prophesied about the birth and death of Jesus. *(Goes over to greet Isaiah.)* Isaiah, I want you to meet my friend, Sam. Sam, this is Isaiah, the Prophet of God.

Isaiah: *(Glares at Sam.)* You look like some of the folks I used to talk to. How many times I said to them, "Awake! Awake! Put on your strength; and they would not hear. Surely he has borne our griefs and carried our sorrows, and still people do not believe." Do you believe? *(Looks straight into the face of Sam.)*

Sam: *(Shifts uncomfortably under the steady gaze of the prophet. Then mutters to himself as he turns away from Isaiah's stare.)* Maybe I'll just open my eyes and make it all go away.

(Music begins to play softly.)

Joe: Come on. The saints are singing. Let's listen.

(Music gradually gets louder as curtain falls and three leave the stage.)

Choir "Surely He Bore Our Grief"
or "Alas! And Did My Savior Bleed"

Scene 3

(Music gradually fades away as curtain rises and Sam and Joe return to the stage.)

Sam: *(Turning slowly toward Joe.)* Is this religious stuff for real, Joe? Is it possible that someone really cares about me enough to bear my griefs and sorrows? I know I am dreaming, but it all seems so real.

Joe: Well, Sam, sometimes it takes the quiet of the night to see reality. It is real, all right. Jesus was here on earth and lived and loved and healed. But even his beloved disciples all left him to seek his own reality in the darkness of the garden.

(Music begins to play softly.)

Sam: Listen, I hear more singing. Who is it this time?

Joe: Let's go see. *(Both begin to walk toward the exit.)* There they are. It is the disciples singing a song of remembrance.

(Music gets louder as curtain falls.)

Choir " 'Tis Midnight And On Olive's Brow"

Scene 4

(Music fades as curtain rises. Joe and Sam are again in Sam's living room.)

Sam: They really took him away and killed him?

Joe: Yes, they really took him and nailed him to the cross. All of nature groaned and cried. Even now all nature tells of how even the birds could find no voice as the Lord hung there that day.

Sam: *(Standing quietly for a few seconds as if trying to control his tears.)* That was awful. And I think I've had a hard day!

Joe: It was a bad day, all right. Joseph and Nicodemus came and took his body and put it in a tomb. The Roman soldiers rolled a stone in front and set the guards to watch over it to make sure no one came to steal the body.

Sam: What happened to him?

(Music begins to play softly.)

Joe: Listen, there are the angels who stood watch. Hear what they say.

(Music increases as curtain falls and Joe and Sam leave stage.)

Choir "The Strife Is O'er, The Battle Done"

Scene 5

(Music fades as curtain rises. Joe and Sam are again in Sam's living room.)

Sam: *(Sounding astonished.)* You mean he wasn't really dead? He just pretended to be dead and left the tomb himself?

Joe: No! No! He was dead. There was no doubt about that.

Sam: But how ...? Why ...?

Joe: It is true. Just like I've been telling you. He is alive and because he is alive, we too can live!

(Mary Magdalene begins running down center aisle toward the stage.)

Sam: Who is that woman running this way?

Joe: That is Mary Magdalene. I think she has just seen Jesus.

(Music begins to play softly.)

Mary M: *(Excitedly, breathing from running hard.)* I have just seen him. I've just seen Jesus. I saw him in the garden. I know he is there and will always walk with me.

(Music increases volume as curtain falls. All leave stage.)

Choir "In The Garden"

Scene 6

(Music fades as curtain rises. Sam and Joe in living room.)

Sam: I don't understand. So what if he rose? What does this have to do with me?

Joe: I don't know about you, Sam, but for me, Jesus is my life.

Sam: Maybe you are right, Joe. Maybe I have been missing something. No, not maybe. I know I have been missing something. I see what you have been trying to get me to see and hear. Jesus really died for me. But he came back from death to give me life.

Joe: I'm glad you are finally beginning to understand, Sam. All our Lord really requires of us is to receive his love and to tell others of his love for them.

Sam: With all my heart I do love him and I want to serve him. Thank you my friend. *(Moves toward Joe with arms open to give him a hug. Joe moves away and off stage before Sam can reach him.)*

Sam: Wait, don't go. I don't want this dream to end.

Joe: *(Calls from off stage.)* It's not a dream, Sam. Open your eyes. It's all real. He is alive!

Sam: *(Looks puzzled. Sits back in his chair, opens his eyes and blinks.)* He is right. Christ is alive. He rose from the grave!

(Jumps up from the chair, picks up phone and dials.) Hey, Joe! It's true! He is alive! Christ is alive!

Choir "Christ The Lord Has Risen Today"
or "Low In The Grave He Lay"

Benediction

Postlude

www.ingramcontent.com/pod-product-compliance
Lightning Source LLC
Chambersburg PA
CBHW071802040426
42446CB00012B/2675